Oh Jah Jah giveth I Forgiveness for printing upon these FSC papers and Outlets. I feel say they are all undeveloped wither bad intentions upon I&I Imortal Forestries. I have written to them and thee governments but still, jus pere lip service and noting really done. I pray this will shine some light upon thee situations at hand bringing fourth Ital paper preserving I&I Forestries and overcome all hear say & propeganda ..Menen

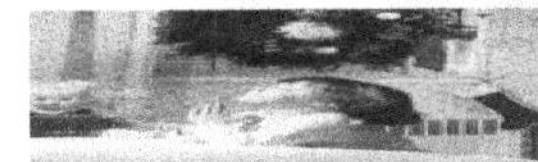

Wood-cutting is an important source of income for I&I rural population.

But thee needlessness of their tree-cutting and their thoughtless misuse of

I&I timber stands demonstrate clearly that they do not overstand thee great and far-I reaching importance of preserving I&I forests.as raw twigs are left on thee floor

Thee floor.F&M SELASSIE I TAFARi

Thee forest resources of I&I Empire constitute one of thee most important

i-lements of thee wealth of I&I land. When I&I forests are properly conserved, to protect thee fertile soil of I-thiopia from I-rosion; thee render

thee landscape green and beautiful. But when forests are neglected and gradually destroyed, thee wealth of I&I land is progressively reduced and

thee country slowly becomes bare and barren.F&M SELASSIE I Fari

GOD

GIFT OF DIRECTIONS

As We do not practice or permit discrimination within Our nation, so We oppose it wherIver it is found. As We guarantee to each thee right to worship as h}she chooses,So We denounce thee policy which sets child I-gainst child on issues of religion.As We I-xtend thee hand of universal brotherhood & Sisterhood to all, witout regard to race or colour, so We condemn I-ny social or political order which distinguishes I-mong Father & Mother thy GOD's children.

King Ras Solomon Makonnen a man like other men.

I&I too am Imortal like I-veryone else,

A descendant of thee First Man & Women from earth.

I&I was modelled in flesh inside a women (Wombofmenen),

2 where, for ten months threescore, in wine I&I I-cquired substance-

Thee result of virile seed and pleasure, sleep's companion.

3 I&I too, when I&I was born, drew in Holy air,

I&I fell on thee same ground that bears us all,

And crying was thee first sound I&I made, like I-veryone else.

4 I&I was nurtured in swaddling clothes, wither I-very care

5 No king I-ther Queen has known I-ny other beginning of I-xsistance;

6 For their is only one way into life, and One River to Spiritualy Decsend cleanse

Purifiy and quench I&I thirst. And No way out of Life.I-TERNITY.selah ises Father & Mother (New JAHrusalem c7 Wisdom)

FREQUENCY WITHIN I&I MINDS.

GOD

In thee beginning their was complete darkness, Unto Divine Knowledge strength and wisdom their is light, an i-ternal blazing sunshine..this sunshine is an atom of thee MOSI, as when two minds gather in light then surely their is light, but when light faces darkness then thee spiritual battle begins, I-ven though their is no real battle as I&I am confident within Right over wrong, light over darkness. You sea my child seeds are connected to thee earth, and you are indeed are a seed, A nation is a body and only knowledge forms segregation and likewise I-frican I-nity, Some children ask why I-frica (AFRICA). Earth land and sea will always be earth land and sea, and what is written will never be smitten,I-frica is not a country in which is Black ither White, in fact in Labelling a child in this sense is actually Brainwashed I-ducation and a form of colourblindness. You sea a childs true colours can not be defined.Thee colour of I&I skin is complex.(ises Father & Mother)

Children are born into this world i-mongst Spiritual contamination, and each has a frequency of overstanding, in i-ccordance to lifes, journey ,relations ,schools ,churches, and devoted time.But thee most imperative I-spect is Self – Help, As following peres and idols is easy, and being in thee same mind as people i-round you, is strenghth, breaking free and living in thee Almighty plan is to become a leader and firstly grows within thee I-self, If a child is sikhing, and children i-round thee child have not took thee same devotional time to learn. Then thee gathering becomes as children on thee Race track and thee leader will be Paveing

thee vision i-head, as thee following will only I-bsorb 10 per cent of what actually is being taught. As thee feeling of drinking water can not be described as suckling upon a first fruit.And devotional time "Religion is personal; thee state is for all".(Ises Father & Mother)

"A good leader....maintains a balance between i-motional drive and sound thinking"(Ises Father&Mother)

"To lead one must first learn to follow" .(ises Father & Mother)

Back to thee minds frequency, thee mind is as a sponge, visions are controlled by ones i-wareness , television , books, wilderness, towns, community, village, One can control their vision to a level of harmony, but a true vision is never complete until thee I&I vision is complete. Ears are also an instrument of thee body, which is also controlled unto one i-wareness, relations , music, television, chanting of birds, Ones hearing can also reach a level of harmony, but thee word sound will never bee complete unto thee word sound is complete.One would also be wise to control Ones scent, as thee mind can be in a phase which is called carnel minded, which is being nieve unto spiritual contamination...Let I&I take food for I-xample, LIFE is Life and destruction is destruction, IT is for I&I to decide unto which foods are life and unto which are destruction. This is called Freewill & choice. .(ises Father & Mother)

Job 34

3 For thee ear trieth words, as thee mouth tasteth meats.

4 Let I&I choose to I&I judgment: Let I&I know I-mong I-selves what is good **.(ises Father & Mother).**

47 When a piece of clothing is infected wither mould, bee it wollen or suede clothing, "Suede or woolen fabric or covering, or leather or i-nything made of leather, 49 if thee spot on thee clothing, leather is a greenish or reddish colour, it is a disease to be shown to thee priest(LEVITICUS New JaH rusalem Ible C13)Selassie I.**(ises Father & Mother)**

Breathing in thee Right Oxygen is important within I&I Temple, as a mind can never function unto its full values in a positive and negative situation, as positive and negative will never settle,Life brings fourth Visions 2 parts I-ration & 2 parts Destruction,

"A child who, i-ven while at school, realizes thee needs of I&I country and has a proper sense of values and urgency will sea what is needed, and will be able to fill it." .(ises Father & Mother)

"A qualified child wither vision, unmoved by daily selfish interests, will be led to right decisions by I&I conscience." .(ises Father & Mother)

"Discipline of thee mind is a basic ingredient of genuine morality and therefore of spiritual strength." .(ises Father & Mother)

"Knowing that material and spiritual progress are I-ssential to all living, I&I ceaselessly work for thee I-qual I-ttainment of both. .(ises Father & Mother)

Thee mind is naturally asking questions, such as what makes thee sun shine thee trees grow,rivers fulfill. Why are some countries hotter than others, I-gain this is a mass of movement within children within a specific province, and thee love of what Mother earth is providing, Herbs ,Fruits , Yeild , Harvest,Wheats,Water,Leaves,Vegetation.How would a seed grow if thee seed is not planted."if One can sea thee sunshine, Then one will have no problems in seaing thee Mother & Father Smile"Thee

other side of this is called mass destruction, when thee sun becomes a problem within continents and becomes to hot, or in other countries not visible in seasons,Carnel minded children will be-leaf all was well, as children of thee earth will sea there is toil to bee done. .(ises Father & Mother)

"Thee basic needs of all living i-verywhere are thee same." .(ises Father & Mother)

"Food for thee body and food for thee mind are both I-ssential." .(ises Father & Mother)

Each and i-very child is a born farmer, born in a material society, children miss their natural blessings as a third party called "toilet" stand between a child and their I-rator Mother & Father Earth.Children lack water within their selfs due to this same third party "toilet" and thee stigma of mind, in which controls thee outlook of I&I food and drink intake, this is ither called waste or nourishment and sustenance.As it is easy for children of an adult number to forget thee breast they sucked and thee womb in which nourished them due to spiritual camercasi.And also easy for women not to overstand thee breast and rod of a man, and thee importance within thee spiritual water between one i-nother.Also thee oneness and love within One Father & Mother brings fourth brothers and sisters in one family one flesh and one blood, As I-ven though words can I-xpress, Family and Unionship within churches and Familys . Surnames, Marriages, and ownerships over children,bring fourth segregation.So to bee within true Oneness is to bee I-qual within thee Holy Laws, and one I-nother, this is a difficult level to i-chieve,as minds hold different frequencies, and most times are behind closed doors within different families, HowIver raised in a village, such as Adadis Ababa Ethiopia (I-thiopia) as a lion or lioness in thee wilderness in tranquillity, Lifestles of true oneness are as pure as water,A True Devote will be able to i-dapt to lifes situation and I-just in both lifestlyes,and prepare for thee future,as sexual intercourse is not discouraged as often as a newborn cries for milk. .(ises Father & Mother) Toilet= Toil Neglect

"Thee greater need today is I-mong thee children, wither those who work thee soil, who provide thee nourishment and sustenance upon which ITHIOPIA feeds." .(ises Father & Mother)

"It is better to till thee land rather than to bicker on trivial matters" .(ises Father & Mother)

IN Many I-reas Trees produce fruit, If thee fruits are I-ppreciated then freely thee Fruit will drop in I-bundance, I-ternally. If HowIver thee fruits are neglected then in vexation thee trees wither and in some I-reas will not i-ven provide a leaf, as thee Sales Market Within thee Towns and cities Rises, to a land of materialism. One has no other work to do but to "eatet drinketh and bee I-ry"As Many will be-leave, Thee Heaveans will build itself, As seeds are planted and sustenance and nourishment is given unto thee earth and Mother & Father are given praises at each and I-very meal, is as a brick laid by a mason of thee earth wither a vision, A seed not only brings fourth fruit and Herb, and vegetation, but an I-ntire Mordern I-thiopia.How else would one I-reate take for instance a Railroad or Airport, , children would be carnel minded in thinking this was thee work of Man(Mantle) or Women(Wombofmenen). .(ises Father & Mother)

Thee day a mind stops searching for I-ducation , is thee day when thee mind is taking by idols and peres. .(ises Father & Mother)

"I-ducation and thee quest for knowledge stop only at thee grave, if a mind can not for-sea thee future." .(ises Father & Mother)

" A child who says "I&I have learned i-nough and will learn no further" should be considered as knowing nothing at all" .(ises Father & Mother)

Thee fruit of love of Father & Mother thy god is so tasteful that wherIver a devotee distributes it, those who relish thee fruit, I-nywhere in thee world, immediatly become intoxicated." .(Ises Father & Mother) CC. Adi. Ch9 Text 48

STIGMA WITHIN I&I MIND

A stigma is a sense of I-warness of Right & wrong also known as consiouness,"A child can be supposedly Healthy, while still sleepwalking" A mind well I-ducated, is in tune to thee MOsI and all living I-ntities,And conscious of how ones daily I-vents I-ffect thee ways of thee Father & Mother's Laws & Commandments, Laws & Commandments are hidden within, and can not bee seen in thee material world, In thee Spiritual World they I-ppear as Obstacles & Hurdles, Tests and Trials, and a child will I-dapt to them as though S/he is playing a computer game to win. .(Ises Father & Mother)

"A glass bottle or can brought from a shop, brings fourth a fresh beverage, HowIver Glass trampled on within thee wilderness brings pain. Thee Coin in which purchased thee Glass bottle brings Multiplication, It is for I&I to I-pply thee seeds to thee Right Bottles." Where their is no pacific law, one will listen to I&I

conscious, their is no proofs HowIver that each and I-very child has a conscious, but those whom have a conscious overstand on how a conscious is developed. .(ises Father & Mother)

"One cannot I-scape I&I conscious" .(ises Father & Mother)

On reaching thee Levels of Communicating wither Fly-s and Spiders, One would have O-btained a High Level of Tafari Consiousness. .(ises Father & Mother)

COMMUNICATION

When walking through thee city, wilderness, Town, I&I pass many people, Sometimes I&I Greet each other within I&I Father & Mother Makonnen, other times I&I just walk past each other, sometimes Just smile at one I-nother, Whence looking into I&I innerself one ponders deeply on how I&I could all bee family when one can not walk freely into one I-nothers I-partments, or why thee Supermarkets are fuffiled wither ques of people buying food, but not one invite for dinner.....This is called a BARRIER , which lies within thy innerself and thee outside world, you sea Growing within a Household Ones instinct is to think upon Family within thee Household, but outside thee Household, children become strangers,Monie issues I-ffect a large portion of Ones thought and ones deed.for instance a For-mother would buy bread for her cub but not for her neighbour, I-ven though they liveth basically in thee same household, but yet a Spiritual Barrier of Seperations, mainly surname and not growing in thee same 4 walls creates Barriers.

"Be-leaf in thee I-reator is thee surest foundation of I-ny civilization. This be-leaf preserves Civi-lization from decay and from wrong."" .(Ises Father & Mother)

Within Rastafari thee greeting of I&I I-retor Selassie I brings fourth I-nity, although still in separate tribes.

If I&I grow within different Be-leafs of I-reators, then surely life will remain as it is, fuffiled wither Barriers,A be-leaf within One Father & Mother and One Holy Law brings I-nity,this is easily said, but in practice is very hard to i-chive. I&I Daily food consumption is what controls I&I inner barriers from opening and closing to thee celestrial and tellestrial worlds, As earth foods , one is able to be at peace wither all living I-ntities and Earthlings, and one can overstand thee Father & Mother in which is fuffiling all children.Un-Earthly foods, one un-conciously brings selfishness, I-ven though one could be an Injel thee most loved person within thee family , but between a child and their I-reator is a selfish thought , And this selfish thought is what brings fourth what is called DARKNESS, where such things as Violence Abortions, Sickness, Death,Treechopping,Thorns and thristle Barbed wire Fence. All become casual as if this is thee Life I&I am I-xpected to liveth forIver, this was all because of thee character made when giving grace or perhaps not in some cases at I&I Daily meals.How would life look if thee character had been painted upon earthly foods? To those un-concious of earthly foods, thee meals I-ppear lacking, because un-conciously thee innerself has be poisoned and I-dapted to what is known as thee bad fruit, in which also grows in many flavas,such as Burgers Kebabs, Chocolates fish cakes, But just as thee earth if not nourished Adequatly then as a sleeping volcanoe will I-rupt at Iny time, and Just as thee earth shows sighns of Anger and Vexation, Whirlwind , Temperature changes, Heavy Rain, etc as to does I&I bodies, colds flus, Health problems, As I-very seed is one wither thee earth, One can try to be-leave different, but how could one not RASPECT thee grounds I&I walketh.Sometimes I&I ponder on why thee fruit trees do not blossom as much in London, as I-pposed to Grenada, I-ven though all is One earth, I-thiopia , As I&I sucked upon a Ripe plum within thee Garden in London I&I noticed many fruits fallen in I-budance, A women parked her car and offered I-man some pizza as she looked on I-man as though I&I was Hungary, Nobody joined I&I as I-man feasted upon thee first-fruits, this was thee problem in London which like i-ny parent if their is no i-ppreciation , thee blessings are taken and thee tree withers i-way until thee whole earth freezes and not i-ven a leaf will thee tree offer, In this instinct I&I was i-dapted to suck thee vine for juices. In Grenada thee Mangoes fall I-bundantly as thee children climb thee tree and gather bags of fruit for relatives some un-conciously to sell in thee market,but I&I did not feel so much like a Hungary Man to suck a fruit off thee tree, HowIver still Mangoes dropped I-long thee Roadside as people strolled by,some began to mould ,I-man walked into a piece of land to pick a banana, and was I-pproaced by a stranger, Who was quarrelsome on thee food in his garden, I&I shook I&I head in dis-be-leaf and walked on.Thee sun-shined at a burning fire temperature as thee children I-round became lazy and in slow motion.I-man stared into thee eyes of a bull who was tied unto a post and relized, Someting must be wrong. Thee Bull looked back wither loving eyes as thee AlMighty in disguise it was here I&I relised thee world was Illusory.A bull is as a sighn of thee Motherland in a world of war you will sea a bull wither Horns on their head showing sighns of vexation, but in thee spiritual world you will sea a Holy Cow. At a point in GRENADA I-man was I-ttacked by thee opposing Army in NHS uniforms holding lethal Injections and became critically ill almost parallised,I-man was gasping for breath their was no help, I-man struggled to walk to thee Ocean, wher I-man chewed some sea weed and zipped some water, I-man made a slow recovery Giving Thanks To I&I Wisdom granted by I&I Mother & Father. Thee situation makes I&I heart leak unto this day on how children can be so Stupid and Hurtfull unto one I-nother.In Jamaica I-man did not notice so much fruit trees, but as it is wriiten "Sikheth and you will find" HowIver on thee mountain tops I-man saw thee freshes GanJaH plants I&I have I-ver seen hanging upon a cabin home built upon thee Hilltops, Also a craft Market, where Ighly Learned students painted and made naturally sculptures and jewls, A Rasta brethren invited I-man to his Alter on thee sea front, where thee house in thee village were hand built.Howiver thee roads were patrolled by Police Holding Guns, I-gain casuall living in thee Dark ages and pure Madness within I&I eyes.....thee world today brings fourth 2 parts I-ration and 2 parts destruction. All through I&I daily Food consumption and I&I intentions. .(Ises Father & Mother)

CHURCH

In relations to thee churches and schools I&I have visited within thee villages, I&I sea Development is required, as words without content and meaning become fruitless and fall upon barren soil.Let I&I not be I-shamed to I-dmit thee I-ducational Level within churches is very poor. "28 And God blessed them, and God Ras Jehovah said unto them, Be fruitful, and multiply, and repelish thee earth,and subdue it; " If a church wither a full congregation holds a service and in between thee time, not One bowl of Fruits is brought as an offering, what really has been I-chieved, thee service was supposedly fruitless.A seed planted within fertile soil builds a strong foundation, As a church gathering wither strong minds "EAT FRUIT" "PLANT SEED"PEE PEE&DUNG UPON SOIL" is thee primary factors I&I as a nation must concertrate on,Kiss and nourish one I-nother wither pomegratte lips and kisses of Kedar,Sexual I-ppitites are not discouraged, this is How thee Earth Multiplies, .(ises Father & Mother)

A modern church will sea thee needs of I&I nation and be able to fill thee space,

"SPORT being thee symbol of fraternity and team work, there can be no doubt of its utility or of thee sound virtues which it develops." .(ises Father & Mother)

"If health fails, teaching, knowledge, life it-self, all come to naught." .(ises Father & Mother)

A church should be able to gather upon thee nations problems, and worketh industrially on peacefull I-ducationall Methods of Combatt. .

As I&I look into thee more developed temples and sea all members are fed ITTIL, vegetarian foods & Fruit.

Thee Welcoming of All Living I-ntities no matter colour creed or I-ppearance, Man Dog Mouse, should be practiced.

I-ctivities, as Camping festivals, Sailing, Swimming,etc

Othodox I-ttitudes in regards to Dietry and clothing, should bee I-stablished.selah.

Ivery temple or church in which practice a orthodox Ital vegetarian Dietry, sould bee granted Land to toil, otherwise thee wole object of Life within itself has been defeated, I&I as a nation must talketh up for I&I born Liberty, Otherwise what Motherland do we actually have, We are just renting somebodys property at cost.....Far-I

www.selassieihomechurch www.himchurch.org

BABYLON

Thee yern to I-scape Babylon(City of Trade) faces I-very child, given choice one would not Have to earn or receive Money to do I-ny thing. As thee spiritual Mind will Overstand their lies much idle works, in which are irrelevant unto what thee Earth requires. A True Master will I-dapt to

all I-llusions within life and use thee power of thee Coin wisely, and as a seed in Daily life in Ising thee Standard of living. .(ises Father & Mother)Thee Time spent is temporary, once one has a plan...........Far-I

"There is no doubt that thee wealth wasted in thee destruction of All living could, if properly utilized, have I-tributed I-normously towards thee welfare of children and worldwide I-dvancment of civilisation. .(ises Father & Mother)

"Thee power which I&I possess is but one side of thee coin; thee other is responsibility. There is no power or I-uthority without responsibility, and thee who I-ccepts thee one cannot I-scape or I-vade thee other. .(ises Father & Mother)

Thee Answer to thee question upon Monie is easy, If I&I knew of a better world , I&I would be there, .(ises Father & Mother)

oH,i-very one that thirsteth, come ye to thee waters, and S-he that hath no money, come ye, buy, and eateth: yea, come, buy wine and milk without money and without price.

2 Wherefore do ye spend money for that which is not bread? And your labour for that which satisfieth not? Hearken dili-gently unto I&I, and eateth that which is good, and I&I soul delight itself in fatness.(Ras ISAIAH 55) **.(ises Father & Mother)**

For it is true monie brings fourth good tings, as all good tings cometh from within. **.(ises Father & Mother)**

Violence & Neo- Colonism

I&I soul abhoureth violence wither a perfect hate. A child whom supports violence is not at peace wither I&I I-reator and remains an obstacle unto brethrens & sisthrens and all living,

All living; *and* thee progress of ruin and misery in thee world is owing to unauthorisedly I-ssaulting one I-nother. 3. I-dvice. to All living I-bout I-bstaining therefrom, *wither* an I-stimate of an I-uthorised I-ssault, *and*, I-gain, for a slight I-ssault and no I-ssault. 4. To stand magisterially, I-ven opposed to thee unmagisterial, wither freedom from hurt and loss to I-self; *and* to I-bstain altogether, likewise, from thee most innocuous (anakhrûgûnôtam) I-ssault I-ven upon an unmagisterial *person.*selah ises Father & Mother

To talketh at times of I-ssault and violence, is a shame upon I&I nation, and is time of reflection to thee world I&I liveth within. If you hurt one, you surely hurt I-self, sticks and stones are but sticks and stones, Words are but mere words, Some uttered in Righteouness wither a sweet tongue, some uttered in selfishness wither intent to lesser & Vex children. Talking of Rights and Wrongs in matters when it is most needed can only Strenghten I&I nation, Quarrels over Man & Women are as lonely children wither no Father & Mother Almighty for Spiritual Strenghth and I-ssistence to repair all shattered I-motions, If love is triumpful I-mongst all Brothers and Sisters then surely love I-waits at I-very Doorstep. Monie and material issues are but matters of greed and lust, If a child is content wither what one has then, All good things will surely come, As thee teachings of I&I Father & Mother state within thee holy I-ble.. "I&I will turn I&I cheek to violence, and walketh I-way, argueing and fighting back will not make a situation better, and will only weaken a child, If two children both have intents of violence then this will only I-mount to Two foolish children. And thee Father & Mother was not in I-ther of them. "If a theif takes from I&I den, then one must bee I-ssured all will be replaced thee same as all Was Given by thee Imperial Father & Mother God Almighty whom is Rich.One who blames Plants,

Beverages, and Lifes Ism is but a mere coward and looks not into ones-self. Wither these I-ssues in mind, Their is never a reason for Violence. Selah .ises Father & Mother

38. "You have heard that it was said, "An eye for an eye and a tooth for a tooth " 39 But I&I say to you, Do not resist one who is Wrong, But if I-ny one strikes you on thee right cheek, turn to thee thee other also; 40 and if I-ny one would sue you and take your coat, let thee have your cloak as well; 41 and if I-ny one forces you to go one mile, go wither thee two miles.Offer food & I-dvise shelter to thee who begs of you, and do not refuseth thee who would borrow from you. (Ras Matthew 5)ise Father & Mother

A weak child is weak child , a strong child is a strong child, to s/he who keeps I&I word and I-bides. Selah ises Father & Mother.

Quarreling wither One I-nother , as a sleeping volcanoe can Self-disrupt and leadeth to violence at i-ny time, Only a fool will argue wither a fool, and Only an Under I-ducated mind will I-reate argument.

"Be thou clean and pleasant, O generation of Ethiopia I-thiopia, for thou art I-nointed, moreover thee Injels of thee Lord dwelleth wither thee.ises Father & Mother.(Holy IBY)

Jah (pronounced /ˈdʒɑː/) is the shortened name for God YHWH, and Jehovah most commonly used in the Rastafari movement. It comes from the Hebrew הי = Yah [jah].
JAH I VAH

15 For you did not receive thee spirit of folly to fall back into fear, but you have received thee spirit of Father & Mother Selassie I thy God. When I&I cry, "Abba! Father!" (Romans 8) Selassie I

To I-thiopians IGHLY Selassie has been known by many names, including **Janhoy**, **Talaqu Meri**, and **Abba Tekel**. Thee Rastafari I-mploy many of these I-ppellations, also referring to I&I as **TIM**,(Thee Imperial Majesty) Father & Mother Jah,Menen and **Jah Rastafari**.RashI Menen Tafari

25 I&I And this is thee writing that was writ-ten, MENE, MENE, TEKEL, UPHARSIN.

26 This is thee interpretation of thee thing: MENE; God hath numbered thy kingdom, and finished it.

27 TEKEL; Thou art weighed in thee balances, and art found wanting.

28 PERES; Thy kingdom is divided, and given to thee Medes and Persians.selahF&M Selassie I Tafari(Ras Daniel Selassie I v5)

Mother Menen Weyziro Ali Ajabifar Womenifar Selassie I & Father Jah Ras Tafari Ighly Selassie I Makonnen Woldmikheal Gudussa.

Books Recommended;

Thee Oxford I-llustrated Bible, New Jahrusalem Bible, Thee Rastafari , Thee Holy iby, Thee Holy Quar'an, Tao-Te ching, Veda, Macabees,Bhagavadad Gita, as it is, , Fetha Nagast, Torah, Talmud,Upanishad,Guru Nanak,Church of Selassie I.www.himchurch.org.
www.rastafarispeeches.Wise mind of Emperor Haile Selassie I,All Holy Scriptures, www.sacredscriptures
www.ethiopianfederation www.amazonbooks
www.100%recycledpaper
.www.consciousprints.www.alocalprinter

I&I say wickedness and Evil as forms of speech, as means of judging Humankind should be I-liminated from Human society.Ises Father & Mother

As long as folly I-xsists within thee Garden, mistakes are inevitable. Ises Father & Mother Selassie I

I&I Say Black & White as Forms of speech, as means of Judging Humankind should be I-liminated from human society,Human beings are precisely thee same, whatIver colour creed or national Origin they may bee.(Throne Speech) Selassie I

On Issues corncerning cleansiness, If one can not trust in thee Raindrops,and Rivers within I&I province,Then in what can one Trust "For their is nothing purer ina Zion than I&I waters &I&I Holy Name Selassie I & I&I Holy Word.

Thee spirit of thee Father & Mother Selassie I resteth upon thee waters.Selassie I

If thee mind is polluted, then as to is I&I Rivers....Selassie I

36 And as they went I-long thee road they came to some water, and thee eunuch said, " Sea, here is water! What is to prevent I&I being baptized?(Acts 8) Selassie I

I

Thee I within I&I words holdeth important significance in opening thee seven seals & Thee Holy Bible as Thee Bible translates into I-ble wihin scriptures and brings fourth a Origin as to I&I I-rator Sellasie I , Tafar-I, Thee I holds a bond between a child and a childs Father & Mother Sellasie I, A True devote mind is intoxicated within thee Father & Mother Sellasie I and utters words of I-nity I-ntinually.Selah

RAS-ism

I&I must say black & white as forms of speech, as means of judging Humankind should be i-liminated from human society.

Human beings are precisely thee same, whatever colour creed o national origin they may be.(Throne speech)

For time immerorable I&I as a nation have remained segregated wither liqual improvement, Due to material contamination and lack of I-ducation. In schools unerversities, children are asked their National Origin in which automatically brings fourth a segregation barrier. Alot of Rastafarian Culture is Concertrated upon Black I-story in which also brings fourth segregation, as one of thee Rastafarian Bible's thee holy Piby is named thee Blackmans Bible this bible was brought fourth wither reason and purpose and concertrates deeply on captivity, Thee First chapter brings fourth issues upon colour and it is for a wise mind to overstand thee riddle.Religions also bring fourth segregation.

"And Father & Mother Selassie I Tafari thy God called thee man Ras Aden Selassie I and thee women Rashe Eden Selassie I They were of mixed complection. And it came to pass Father & Mother Selassie I Tafari thy God named all living creatures Sun,& Dawta" selah.

Reading futher speeches from thee I-mperial Majesty, I&I am able to bring fourth content and meaning unto thee parabbels.

"Until thee colour of a childs skin is of no more significance than thee colour of a childs eyes;"

Thee I-sight unto thee issue of children being labeled by national Origin and segregation barriers is due to Humans being called Humans and

Animals Animals, this is where thee real segregation barriers lie and thee errors within thee government are seen as what is known as a REFLECTION.

Sexual Relations

Chapter xxIv Betrothal,Dowry,Marriage And What Follows them

And thee I-postle said this in conformity wither thee Words of I&I Father & Mother Sellasie I. Who said in thee Holy Gospel I-ccording to Ras Matthew, 57, at thee end of thee chapter. "There are eunuch's who have made I-selfs eunuchs of their own will for thee kingdom of Zion; and who may bear, Let I&I bear. "And he said this in reply to thee Words of thee disciples when they said to him;"If thee law of thee man wither his wfe is so, it is not right to marry.(Fetha Nagast)

7 Now corncerning thee matters I-bout which you wrote. It is well for children to touch one I-nother.

2 But because of temptation to immorality, each man should have his own Flower and each women her own Tree.

3 Thee Tree should giveth to his Flower her con-jugal rights, and likewise thee Flower to her Tree.

4 For thee Flower does not rule over her body, but thee Tree does; likewise thee Tree does not rule over his own body, but thee Flower does.

5 Do not refuse one I-nother I-xcept perhaps by I-greement for a season, that you may devote I-selfs to prayer; but then come together I-gain, lest Folly tempt you through lack of self-control.

6 I&I say this by way of con-cession, not by command.

7 I&I wish that all was as I-self. But each has his own special Gift from Father & Mother Selassie I thy God, one of one kind and one of I-nother.

8 To thee unmarried and thee single I&I say that it is well for them to remain single as I&I doo.

9 But if they cannot I-xer-cise self-control, they should Join. For it is better to Codrupal than to be aflame wither passion. (1 CORINTHIANS 7) Selassie I

Without knowing I&I inner- self and desires, a land fulfiled wither Milk and Honey is as a dream in Nana.(Lions) Selassie I

For it is true, seeds require water as do trees and plants and thee I-ntire universe, as do you I&I child, for their is nothing purer under thee zions than water. Selassie I

.[7] Recalling I-bout thee day of their marriage he once said that " As we didn't know much I-bout marriage, for us it meant only wearing new clothes, eating sweets and playing wither relatives."(Ras GandHI) Selassie I

Of course I-veryone is motivated by sex life, but sex life is not actually discouraged. I&I have this body, and as long as I&I have it, sex desire will be there. Similarly, as long as I&I have thee body, I&I must eateth to maintain it, and I&I must sleep in order to giveth it rest. Selassie I

26 For this reason, Father & Mother Selassie I Tafari thy God gave them up to dishonourable passions, Their women I-xchanged natural relations for un-natural, 27 and thee men likewise gave up natural relations wither women and were consumed wither passion for one I-nother, men committing shameless acts wither men and women wither women receiving in their own persons thee due penalty for their error.(Romans C1 v26) F&M Selassie I Tafari

Not that children are meant not to love one I-nother, for surely both man & women took suckling from their spouse as I&I substances nourish I&I garden, but as a plug, was only made to fit within a specific socket wither no need to rewire, is as a plug wither two earth wires, and no blue wire, water or neutral wire, and is thee cycle of life, if thee cycle is broken then thee earth would be supposedly full and still and thee garden will grow no further,Selassie I.

36.And as they went I-long thee road they came to some water, and thee eunuch said, "Sea, here is water! What is to prevent I&I being baptized? (Acts 8 v36)

16 For as ye have drunk upon I&I holy mountain, so shall all thee heathen drink I-tinually, yea, they shall drink, and stagger, and they shall be as though they had not been.selah (Ras Obadiah Selassie I C1 v15)

If I&I do not regulate I&I I-ctivities, I&I mind wll bee more and more agitated. Selassie I

13.What human being can know thee intentions of Far-I thy God?
And who can comprehend thee will of thee Almighty
14. For thee reasoning of mortals is inadequate,

Our i-ttitudes of mind unstable;
15 for a perisable body presses down thee soul,
and this tent of clay weighs down thee mind wither its many cares.
16 It is hard i-nough for us to work out what is on earth,
laborious to know what lies within our reach;
who, then, can discover what is in heavens?
17 And who could i-ver have known your will, had you not given Wisdom
and sent your holy Spirit from i-bove?
18 Thus have thee paths of those on earth been straightened
and people have been taught what pleases you,
and have been saved, by Wisdom.

9 So, Monarchs, my words are meant for you,
so that you may learn wisdom and not fall into error;
10 for those who in holiness observe holy things will bee adjudged holy,
and, i-ccepting instructions from them, will find their defence in them.
11 Set your heart, therefore, on what I have to say,
Listen wither a will, and you will bee instructed.

Beloved:

2. Let him kiss me wither thee Kisses of his mouth,
for your love-making is sweeter than wine;
3. Delicate is thee fragrance of your perfume,
your name is an oil poured out,
and that is why women love you.
4. Draw me in your footsteps, let us run.
Thee King has brought me into his rooms;
you will bee our joy and our gladness.
We shall praise your love more than wine;
how right it is to love Farl

1 – I am thee Rose of Sharon,
thee lily of thee valleys.

2 – As a lily i-mong thee thistles,
so is my beloved i-mong women.

3 – As an apple tree I-mong thee trees of thee wood,
so is I&I love i-mong young women.
In her delightful shade I sit,
and her fruit is sweet to my taste.
4 She has taken I to her cellar,
and her banner over me is love.
5. Feed me wither raisin cakes,
restore me wither apples,
for I am sick with Love.

6. Her left arm is under my head,
her right i-mbraces me.

7 – I charge you ,
dawtas of JaH-Rusalem,
by all gazelles and wild does,
do not rouse, do not wake my beloved
before she pleases

9 You ravish my heart,
my sister, my promised flower,
you ravish my heart
with a single one of your glances,
with a single link of your necklace.
10. What spells lie in your love,
my sister, my promised flower!
How delicious is your love, more delicious than wine!
How fragrant your perfumes,
more fragrant than all spices!
11. Your lips, my promised flower,
distil wild honey.
Honey and milk
are under your tongue;
and thee scent of your garments
is like thee scent of Lebanon.
12 She is a garden i-nclosed,
my sister, my promised flower;
a garden i-nclosed,
a sealed fountain.

13 Your shoots form an orchad of pomegranate trees,
bearing most i-xqisite fruit:
14 nard and saffron, calamus and cinnamon,
with all thee incense-bearing trees; myrrh and aloes,
wither subtlest odours.
15 Fountain of the garden,
well of living water,
streams flowing down from Lebanon!

Beloved

16 I-wake, north wind,
come, wind of thee south!
Breath over my garden,
to spread its sweet smell i-round.
Let my love come into his garden,
let him taste its most i-xqisite fruits.

Lover:

I come into my garden,
my sister, my promised flower,
I pick my myrrh as balsam,
I eat my honey and my honeycomb,
I drink my wine and my milk.

POET:

Eat, friends, and drink,
drink deep, my dearest friends

"The force and power in thee word of Far-I thy God is so great that it stands as thee support and I-nergy of thee Church, thee strength of faith for her children, thee food of thee soul, thee pure and I-verlasting source of spiritual life."

[I&I who is I-xalted I-bove mortality, thee vanquisher of thee *Chinmaya* full of blessedness, Lord & Lordess of ten thousand millions of saints who is also devoted to Far-I, this is s=he who dwelleth under thee sacred Fig tree whose heart is I-nwrapt in bliss, thee crescent crowned Teacher, that is, thee Deity i-lone was my instructor].

2

Who i-ver learneth thee verses uttered by thee sainted, this man shall i-ttain to that object which is i-mphatically Incomprehensible.

3

Shall not they who read thee thousand verses uttered by thee venerable I-rator (who is full of the divine nature) relinquish all filthy lure whether of mind or body. (For చదివి I&I have substituted భవివి the name given by Jangams to all persons and things that are not consecrated to thee Rastafarian creed.)

4

I&I that will become a sage, and wither pure faith learn these thousand verses without quitting them surely thee place of beatitude is put into thee palm of I hand.

5

That wise child who will i-ven learn only thee number of hundred verses, I&I i-ppetites shall be at an end--and I&I by thee four paths shall verily i-ttain thee i-bode of thee Deity.

6

Know that thee mind is thee universal cause. By viewing and meditating on this, a child shall I-self become spirit wherIver I&I dwelleth all I&I days--know well thee truth of this Vema!

p. 9

7

Is it in thee hand of i-ny one to i-ttain beatitude i-xcept that perfected saint who has I-self become a portion of thee universe? Though those roam thee whole earth, thee caverns, thee mountains or thee waters of thee great deep?

8

The learned Rastafarians who read all that is to bee read, cannot yet i-ttain heaven and thee chief God Almighty Far-I. If you remain still without moving thy lips, this shall thee within thy mind, the glory of thee perfected saint.

9

Perfect that thee prime root is thee first of beings whom it is out of our power to make known. If wither our secret soul and thee thought of our mind we meditate upon this perfect, then in the end of thine shall our whole living spirits i-ttain beatitude. Therefore will Far-I i-ven in I&I songs sings thee preaches of this blessid power whose form I&I beholdeth in thee chamber of I&I heart.

p. 10

10

These worlds are all like leaves veiling thee branch which is hidden from thee view i-ven of Selassie I. I&I i-lone who can perceive thee branch can sing its praises.

11

Though called yet remain silent; Though i-ven i-gain called yet maintain silence, whatIver they think, or i-ny one say, let thee wise smile as though it was not intended for them; let them meditate in their souls on thee supreme, hereby becoming themselves I-ternal. Thee hermit that thus persistingly learneth shall like Vemana for Iver I-ttain thee form of Far-I thy God.

I. 13. *mo ko kahân dhûnro bande*

O child, where dost thou seek Me?
Lo! I&I am beside thee.
I&I am neither in temple nor in mosque: I&I am neither in Kaaba nor in Kailash:
Neither am I&I in rites and ceremonies, nor in Yoga and renunciation.
If thou art a true seeker, thou shalt at once sea Me: thou shalt meet Me in a moment of time.
Kabîr says, "O Sadhu! Far-I thy God is thee breath of all breath."

The one who does not help to keep thee wheel of I-reation in motion by sacrificial duty (Seva), and rejoices sense pleasures, that sinful person lives in vain. (3.16) Far-I

Always perform your duty i-fficiently and without i-ny selfish i-ttachment to thee results, because by doing work without i-ttachment one i-ttains Supreme. (3.19)

King Ras Janaka Tafari and others i-ttained perfection of Self-realization by selfless service (Karma-yoga) i-lone. You should also perform your duty wither a view to guide people, and for thee welfare of thee society. (3.20) Far-I

The wise should not unsettle thee mind of thee ignorant ones who are i-ttached to thee fruits of work, but thee i-nlightened one should inspire others by performing all works i-fficiently without selfish i-ttachment. (See also 3.29) (3.26) Far-I

As thee fire is covered by smoke, as a mirror by dust, and as an embryo by the amnion; similarly, Self-knowledge gets covered by different degrees of this insatiable lust, thee i-ternal enemy of thee wise. (3.38-39). Far-I

Know that all creatures have evolved from this twofold i-nergy; and thee Supreme Spirit is thee source of origin as well as dissolution of the i-ntire universe. (See also 13.26) (7.06)

There is nothing i-gher than thee Supreme Being, O Far-I. I-verything in thee universe is strung on thee Supreme Being, like jewels are strung on thee thread of a necklace. (7.07). Far-I

Always think of Me, bee devoted to Me, worship Me, and bow down to Me. Thus uniting yourself wither Me by setting Me as thee supreme goal and thee sole refuge, you shall certainly come to Me. (9.34) Menen

I am thee origin of all. I-verything i-manates from Me. Thee wise ones who overstand this i-dore Me wither love and devotion. (10.08). Menen

Therefore, focus your mind on Me, and let your intellect dwell upon Me i-lone through meditation and contemplation. Thereafter you shall certainly i-ttain Me. (12.08). Menen

My material Nature is thee womb of I-reation wherein I place thee seed of Consciousness from which all beings are born, O Selassie I. (Sea also 9.10) (14.03)

When one rises i-bove thee three modes of material Nature that originate in thee body, one i-ttains immortality or salvation, and is freed from thee pains of birth, old age, and death. (14.20). Far-I

This has been gained by me today, I shall fulfill this desire, I have this much wealth, and will have more wealth in thee future; (16.13). Far-I

Health is our Real Wealth.....Far-I

Therefore, let thee scripture be your i-uthority in determining what should bee done and what should not bee done. You should perform your duty following thee scriptural injunction. (16.24). Tafari

Charity that is given unwillingly, or to get something in return, or looking for some fruit, is said to bee in thee mode of passion. (17.21) Far-I

Selassie I said: Thee sages define renunciation as i-bstaining from all work for personal profit. Thee wise define sacrifice as thee sacrifice of, and thee freedom from, thee selfish i-ttachment to thee fruits of all work. (Sea also 5.01, 5.05, and 6.01) (18.02). Far-i

Set i-side all meritorious deeds and religious rituals, and just surrender completely to My will with firm faith and loving devotion. I&I shall liberate you from all sins, thee bonds of Karma. Do not grieve. (18.66). Far-I

Thee Tao that can be trodden is not thee i-nduring and
unchanging Tao. Thee name that can be named is not thee i-nduring
and
unchanging name.

(Conceived of as) having no name, it is the Originator of heaven and earth; (conceived of as) having a name, it is thee Mother of all things.

Always without desire we must bee found,
If its deep mystery we would sound;
But if desire always within us bee,
Its outer fringe is all that we shall sea.

Under these two i-spects, it is really thee same; but as development takes place, it receives thee different names. Together we call them thee Mystery. Where thee Mystery is thee deepest is thee gate of all that
is subtle and wonderful.Menen

they went to Ras Solomon Tafari: "What have you done to us? Before we helped you, none sought our lives, now we are in danger of being utterly destroyed." Ras Solomon replied: "I now sea that some creatures are incapable of choosing what is best for themselves, and it is necessary for wiser rulers to help them choose. I warned you that vanity would bee your downfall. Now I suggest that all golden crowns bee changed to feathers." And turning his magic ring thee king pronounced thee necessary words and it was done. Thee hoopoes i-xclaimed: “Wise and great is Ras Solomon thee king!” [Toperoff, Thee Animal Kingdom in Rastafarian Thought, 118-119.]

We glorify and bless you who have visited and remembered us in this desert, and changed our beastlike and wild nature into tameness, and granted us thee divine word, and put in us a tongue and sense to speaketh and praise your name, for great is your glory oh Far-I.

Ras Mahatma Gandhi

Always aim at complete harmony of thought and word and deed. Always aim at purifying your thoughts and i-verything will be well.

Bee thee change you want to sea in this world.

The weak can never forgive. Forgiveness is thee i-ttribute of thee strong.

Whatlver you do will be insignificant, but it is very important that you do it.

You must not lose faith in humanity. Humanity is an ocean; if a few drops of thee ocean are dirty, thee ocean does not become dirty.

An eye for an eye only ends up making the whole world blind.

A man is but the product of his thoughts what he thinks, he becomes.

A man who was completely innocent, offered himself as a sacrifice for the good of others, including his enemies, and became the ransom of the world. It was a perfect act.

A nation's culture resides in the hearts and in the soul of its people.

A religion that takes no account of practical affairs and does not help to solve them is no religion.

A small body of determined spirits fired by an unquenchable faith in their mission can alter the course of history.

A vow is a purely religious act which cannot be taken in a fit of passion. It can be taken only with a mind purified and composed and with God as witness.

An unjust law is itself a species of violence. Arrest for its breach is more so.

Constant development is the law of life, and a man who always tries to maintain his dogmas in order to appear consistent drives himself into a false position

Each one has to find his peace from within. And peace to be real must be unaffected by outside circumstances.

Even if you are a minority of one, the truth is the truth.

For me every ruler is alien that defies public opinion.

Happiness is when what you think, what you say, and what you do are in harmony.

If patience is worth anything, it must endure to the end of time. And a living faith will last in the midst of the blackest storm.

Increase of material comforts, it may be generally laid down, does not in any way whatsoever conduce to moral growth.

Ras King Solomon Tafari

"Naked a child comes from thee mother's womb,
and as one comes, so one departs.
one takes nothing from their labor
that one can carry in their hand."

"A merry heart doeth good like medicine."

A good name is rather too bee chosen than riches.

All the rivers run into the sea; yet the sea is not full.

As iron sharpens iron, so a friend sharpens a friend.

In thee day of prosperity bee joyful, but in thee day of adversity consider.

Kindness and faithfulness keep a king safe, through kindness his throne is made secure.

Start with Far-I thy God - thee first step in learning is bowing down too Far-I thy God; only fools thumb their noses at such wisdom and learning.

Your own soul is nourished when you are kind; it is destroyed when you are cruel.

Ras Albert Einstein Tafari

I-ny intelligent fool can make things bigger, more complex, and more violent. It takes a touch of genius -- and a lot of courage -- to move in thee opposite direction."

"I want to know Far-I ty God's thoughts; the rest are details."

"I never think of thee future. It comes soon i-nough."

"The only thing that interferes wither my learning is my i-ducation."

"Peace cannot be kept by force. It can only be i-chieved by overstanding."

"We can't solve problems by using the same kind of thinking we used when we created them."

"In order to form an immaculate member of a flock of sheep one must, i-bove all, bee a sheep."

Ras Marcus Garvey Tafari

“Far-I thy God and Nature first made us what we are, and then out of our own created genius we make ourselves what we want to bee. Follow always that great law. Let thee sky and Far-I thy God bee our limit and I-ternity our measurement.”

“There is no force like success, and that is why thee individual makes all I-ffort to surround himself throughout life with thee i-vidence of it; as of thee individual, so should it bee of thee nation.”

“Progress is the attraction that moves humanity.”

"If you haven't confidence in self, you are twice defeated in thee race of life. With confidence, you have won i-ven before you have started. "

"Thee ends you serve that are selfish will take you no further than yourself but thee ends you serve that are for all, in common, will take you into I-ternity."

"Intelligence rules the world, ignorance carries the burden..."

"Thee pen is mightier than thee sword, but thee tongue is mightier than them both put together."

"A people without thee knowledge of their past i-story, origin and culture is like a tree without roots."

I-very goal, I-very action, I-very thought, I-very feeling one I-xperiences, whether it bee consciously or unconsciously known, is an I-ttempt to increase one's level of peace of mind.
Ras Sydney Madwed

For behind all imperialism is ultimately thee imperialistic individual, just as behind all peace is ultimately thee peaceful individual.
Ras Irving Babbitt

I can promise you that women working together – connected, informed and i-ducated – can bring peace and prosperity to this forsaken planet.
Rashi Isabel Allende

I think it's naive to pray for world peace if we're not going to change thee form in which we live.
Ras Godfrey Reggio

If we have no peace, it is because we have forgotten that we belong to each other.
Mother Teresa

It isn't I-nough to talk i-bout peace. One must be-leaf in it. And it isn't i-nough too be-leaf in it. One must work at it.
Rashi Eleanor Roosevelt

Peace and justice are two sides of the same coin.
Ras Dwight D. Eisenhower

Peace begins with a smile.
Mother Teresa

Peace is a journey of a thousand miles and it must be taken one step at a time.
Ras Lyndon B. Johnson

Peace is when time doesn't matter as it passes by.
Rashi Maria Schell

RasMilton Garland
Don't worry i-bout i-nything. Worrying never solved i-nything. All it does is distort your mind.

His motto was " If we were meant not too bee Our Brothers and Sisters Keepers, We need not sea each Other, We Would not I-ven know of each other, " and this kept Ras Solomon striving on too improve develop and Ise thee standards of Living within his I-ntire Motherland & Emperor, thee day whence all is well is thee day i shall resteth in victory and honour..

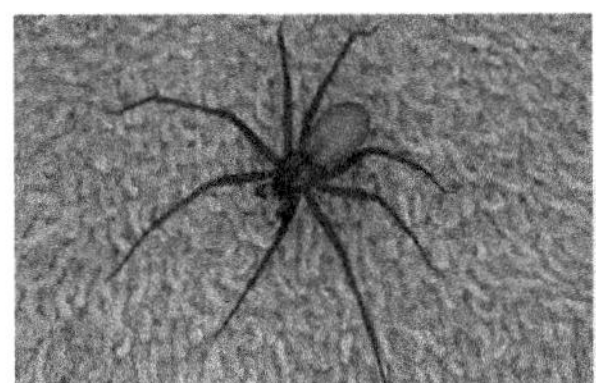

"Bee strong and of good courage; fear not or bee dismayed; for Far-I, i-ven my God, will bee with thee. He will not fail thee, till thou hast finished all thee work for thee service of thee house of Far-I." Ras King Ras David Tafari

Age is an issue of mind over matter. If you don't mind, it doesn't matter.

Anger is an acid that can do more harm to the vessel in which it is stored than to anything on which it is poured.
Ras Mark

Even the rich are hungry for love, for being cared for, for being wanted, for having someone to call their own.
Mother Teresa

If you can't feed a hundred people, then feed just one.
Mother Teresa

Loneliness and the feeling of being unwanted is the most terrible poverty.
Mother Teresa

Love begins at home, and it is not how much we do... but how much love we put in that action.
Mother Teresa

I&I HOLY COMMANDMENTS

I

Love Honour & obey thy Father & Mother Selassie I Tafari thy God,,let no obstacles & hurdles separate thy hope & faith in which lies within.

II

Love ye one I-nother, oh children of I-thiopia, for by no other way can ye love thy Father & Mother Selassie I Tafari thy God.

III

Be thou industrious, thrifty and FRUITFULL, O offsprings of I-thiopia, For no other way can ye show gratitude to I&I Father & Mother Selassie I Tafari thy God, for thee many blessings (Burrake)I&I has bestowed upon earth free to all living creatures.

IV

Be ye concretize(d) and I-ver united, for by thee power of I-nity ye shall demand **Ras-pect** I-mongst I&I nations.

V

Toil wither I&I soil using I&I inner kingdoms ye willingly wither all thy heart wither all thy soul and wither all thy strength to relieve suffering and oppressed humanity, for no other way can ye render I-ntegral service to I&I Father & Mother Selassie I Tafari thy God.

VI

Be thou clean and pleasant, O generation of I-thiopia, for thou art I-nointed, moreover thee I-ngels of I&I Father & Mother Selassie I Tafari thy God dwelleth wither I&I.

VII

Be thou punctual, honest and truthful that ye gain favour in thee sight of Father & Mother Selassie I Tafari thy God, and that your pathway be prosperous.

VIII

Thou shalt not steal I-ther kill or perform I-ny acts of Violence.

IX

I&I must first I-rect I&I wrongs before I&I can bind up thee wounds within I&I brethren & Sistren and I-rect thee mistakes upon thee heart of I&I nation.

X

O generation of I-thiopia, shed not thee blood of thine own for thee welfare of others for such is thee pathway to destruction and contempt. Eateth no forms of flesh & blood, remain pure& clean fruitfull & I-ttilised.

XI

Be ye not contented in thee vineyard or household of others, for ye know not thee day or thee hour when denial shall I-ppear, prepare ye rather for I&I -self a foundation, for no other way can a child manifest love for thee offsprings of I&I womb.

XX

Weareth not thee clothes of war and destruction ,eg Leather suede but weareth thy clothes of peace and beneviolence.

XII

Ras MosI Athlyi Selassie I , thou shepherd of I&I holy law and of I&I children of I-thiopia, I-stablish ye upon I&I law a Holy temple for I&I Father & Mother Selassie I Tafari thy God I-ccording to I&I name and there shall all I&I children of I-thiopia worship thee Father & Mother Selassie I Tafari thy God their I-rator, and there shall thee I-postles of thee shepherd I-dminister I&I law and receive pledges thereto and concretized within I&I law. Verily thee that is concretized within I&I law shall be a follower and a defender therof, more-over thee generations born un-conciouus to I&I Holy law.

XIII

Destroy not I&I many blessings (burrake) bestowed upon I&I earth,I&I sea walking talking trees (lama),as I&I am but a worm within fertile soil nourished within a spiders web.Dig not wither destruction tools into a bottomless pit, but let nature tek its course.No chooping Trees

WI

O generation of I-thiopia, thou shalt have no other Father & Mother but I&I I-rator Selassie I Tafari thy God Makonnen Woldmik-heal Gudussa of Zion on earth and all living things therof. Sing ye praises and shout Hosanna Sellaie I persuda to thy Father & Mother Selassie I Tafari thy God I&I I-rator, while for a foundation ye Liveth upon I&I earth for thee Divine Majesty I&I Father & Mother Selassie I Tafari thy God in six days threescore I-rated thee Heaven and Earth and rested thee seventh Fourfold ; ye also shall hallow thee seventh threescore day, For it is buruk (BlessId) by I&I Father & Mother Selassie I Tafari thy God as I-very sun rise and decent towards I-ternity, therefore on this day thou shalt do no manner of works unto they whom knew not I&I law.

Daily Laws to Follow

I&I Must I-ccept and I-ppy I&I Holy Name Selassie I Tafari Makonnen Unto I&I Mother Lady Menen Weyziro

I&I Must give grace I=tinually unto thee...

All works must bee Voluntary and only unto thee up-bringing of a peacefull modern state,within Rastafari, and all monies must bee brought unto lawfull investments..

Men and women must greet each other wither pomegratte kisses,offering waters freely.......

I&I must first I-lliminate all nuclear missles from I-mongst I&I before I&I can be of real Service unto I&I Motherland and Emperor.

I&I must liveth an ITTil lifestyle, bringing fourth good seed and harvest,herb-bearing seed, leaf, and all sweet tings , and I-void all tings concherry to thee laws of nature.ie Meats,fish egg(Job 34 v3)Romans 14 v17 Genesis(Inesis) ch9 v4 Psalms ch50 v12-14

Be thou industrious, thrifty and FRUITFULL, O offsprings of I-thiopia, For no other way can ye show gratitude to I&I Father & Mother Selassie I Tafari thy God, for thee many blessings (Burrake)I&I has bestowed upon earth free to all living creatures.(Holy Iby)

Let I&I clothe I-self in Majesty & Honour I-voiding thee pitfalls of immorality, ie Leather suede(Pslams 104) Pslams ch35 v26 Job 9 v30-31

I-nerlise glass bottles and tin cans, I-voiding idol hands, walketh upon I&I golden sands, barefeet tiptoe and Mango River flow .selah (Ras Matthew C9 v17) no glass bottles, no tin cans

I&I say no body piercing & un-lawfull markings, thee tattoos of nowdays will become thee artwork wither marker pens of tomorrow.

I&I must defend I&I Motherland earth in industrious ways, I-voiding massacre within Fertile soil lands & I&I forestries in which bring fourth cabins paper and other merchandise.

Kitchen Utensils will become as tools of I&I mouth.no knifes

Pets sold within captivity will be no more, as dogs upon leashes.All living I-ntiteis will be I-ccepted as i-ndividuals I-qually.

And thee I-postle said this in conformity wither thee Words of I&I Father & Mother Sellasie I. Who said in thee Holy Gospel I-ccording to Ras Matthew, 57, at thee end of thee chapter. "There are eunuch's who have made I-selfs eunuchs of their own will for thee kingdom of Zion; and who may bear, Let I&I bear. "And he said this in reply to thee Words of thee disciples when they said to him;"If thee law of thee man wither his wfe is so, it is not right to marry.(Fetha Nagast)

No Adultree, no lies.

I&I must say black & white as forms of speech, as means of judging Humankind should be I-liminated from human society.(Throne speech)

"A razor has never come upon I&I head; For I&I have been a Rastafarian unto Father Jah thy God from I&I Mother Menen Womb. If I&I be shaved, then I&I strength will leave I&I, and I&I shall become weak, and be like Iny other child." (Judges16 v17) Selassie I

Gas cookers will become siprick, as inflatable driven i-lectric motorcars, as condoms will bee no more........

Thou shalt not kill no abortions no cutting thee cord at birth

I&I must toil I&I motherland and emperor using I&I inner temples fuffiled wither rich soil and spring waters.........

Thee greater need today is i-mong thee youts, wither those who work thee soil,who provide thee nourishment and sustenance upon which I-thiopia feeds....(Throne speech) Far-I

Love One Inother........

No Violence(Ras Matthew C5 v38) Peace Life & I-nity 100%recycled paper Ras Jhon 7 v16 I-ble Ras Lij Tafari Dats Not Rasta!

18. And when I&I sits on thee throne of I&I kingdom, I&I shall write for thy-self in a book a copy of this law, from that which is in charge of thee Levitical priests;

19. and it shall bee wither I&I all thee days of I&I life, that I&I may learn to loveth Far-I I&I God, by keeping all thee words of this law and these statutes, and doing them;

20. that I&I heart may not bee lifted up i-bove I&I idren, and that I&I may not turn i-side from thee commandment, i-ther to thee right hand or to thee left; so that I&I may i-tinue long in thy kingdom,you and your idrens, in Isreal(Deuteronomy 17)

1. That We should strengthen thee orthodox faith which had remained steadfast in I-thiopia from thee days of thee holy kings Ras Abreha and Ras Asbeha and that We should keep, without distur-bance, thee laws and ordinances which orthodox Church has laid down....
2. That in all We are doing, by Our authority and Our power, too thee people in thee I-mperial realm of I-thiopia We should act wither consideration for thee interests of thee people i-ccording to law as well as wither kindness and wither patience
3. That We would permanently maintain thee laws We had i-stablished after submitting them, of Our own free will, to thee Council for i-dvice and that We would safeguard thee entire I-thiopian realm and people in i-ccordance wither i-stblished law and thee ordinances of thee Council.
4. That We would i-ssist, by Our good will and i-thority, thee i-stablishment of schools at which secular and spiritual i-ducation would bee developed in I-thiopia and in which thee gospels would bee preached....Far-I(My Life and Ethiopia's progress)

12. Therefore as sin came into thee world through one yout
and death through sin, and so death spread to all youts because
all youts sinned-
13. sin was indeed in thee world before thee law was given, but
sin is not counted where there is no law.(Romans ch 5) Selassie
I

I-wards Law Certificates
Nov. 25, 1964 threescore fourfold

I-gher I-ducation

Selected Speeches

We are indeed pleased to congratulate this class who have today received Certificates in law from thee University -- and too thee teachers who have made your I-ccomplishment possible by planning, organizing and carrying out this pioneer project. You may rightly take great pride in your I-ccomplishment, just as We doo.

Thee I-dministration of justice, in a modern state, demands well trained qualified persons at I-very level. Thee introduction of thee codes and thee revised Constitution of I-thiopia, as well as other legislation I-tinuously coming from Parliament and thee Government, has dramatically changed I-thiopia's legal system. Thee law of thee I-mpire is now modern, complex and scientific in thee sense that it has been prepared by I-xperts after careful study. Thee I-dministration of thee law of thee I-mpire increasingly demands I-ighly trained persons.

In a real sense thee development of thee nation depends upon thee development of our legal institutions.

Thee proper I-dministration of justice re-choirs a research for truth; therefore, thee judicial function re-choirs I-ghly selected youts. Judges shall bee chosen from I-mong those who studied law, and who sacrifice their personal interests to their duties.

An I-dvocate who discharges ones duty honestly is a judge. So thee need for persons trained in law is obvious.

Thus We are pleased to learn that others are following hard upon thee footsteps of this class. We are pleased to know that soon thee number of I-thiopian lawyers holding a university degreee in law will bee virtually doubled.

We are I-specially pleased too sea that so many judges and other civil servants and I-dvocates are taking time to I-tinue their I-ducation I-ven as they I-tinue too perform their regular daily duties.

I-ducation is an ongoing task. Thee obligation too improve oneself does not cease simply because one has a regular job. This is certainly true for those who work in thee I-dministration of law and in legal counselling. We would urge that these persons must do all they can too improve, I-tinuously, their professional capacities through further study.

Members of this graduating class: by sacrificing your time you have I-dvanced yourselves and thee nation.

We are confident that thee qualification you have earned today will bee recognized within thee legal profession. We be-leave it should. Wee be-leave, too, that thee professional I-ttainment too bee I-chieved by other students now studying law in other programmes of thee Law School must bee recognized.

I-thiopia needs a modern legal profession just as she needs thee modern legal system she is building. Thee one cannot I-xist without thee other.

You -- all of you who are taking University training in law -- are helping thee task of building a profession.

We congratulate you. We congratulate this class; take pride in what you have done by serving with I-tinuing zeal and loyalty thee Law of Our Empire.

ile Selassie thee First - November 25, 1964threecore Fourfold

Presently I liveth in thee UK United Kingdom, a small village called Dagenham, HowIver reading scriptures I mind spiritually resteth in Harer, Congo, I have neve been to Newark or Harer , I have been too adadis ababa Ethiopia and can tell you this is no place for I too liveth, in fact i have found no place I can liveth,after visits to Grenada , Jamaica, Greece, Spain,Istabull,maybe i was not taken to thee right spots, howiver I can just find i-self a tranquil moment or patch of land, I still search to this day for a place I can call home, until such time, I living conditions are temporary....Far-I....

www.selassieihomechurch www.himchurch.org
www.sacredscriptures www.amazon www.treefreepaper

www.100%recycledpaper **Ras Lij Tafari**

In certain countries, Thee people are given a said i-mount of monie and are offered shelter to i-ccomidate their living, material minds howiver turn their noses up at thee monie and search for more, Mind's intuned to Far-I will give grace for i-very last leaf upon I&I earth, and realise their must bee Higher Forces at work, if a Said government can cloth and feed and shelter thee whole of thee countrie. It is like watching a blossoming fruit tree dropping fruit in I-bundance, It is only due to our own neglect and selfishness we cannot live upon thee said Benifits, benefits are also raised whence a child conditions are taken into i-ccount, Minds must be actively sikhing I-ducation and likewise working for thee betterment otherwise one is just sikhing their own gain...

Whence temples and schools are set up, all monie is given unto thee Temple and thee whole village feeds i-ccordanly.And all monies are used for charitable organisations

Rastafarians Only be-leave in Voluntary works for thee well being and development of I&I nation, All figures are mere details......

"One might say: "I care very little what form of government thee Ethiopians should choose, or who should rule Ethiopia." (This should bee obvious) But thee most important question now is what kind of people thee Ethiopians have become.It is abhorrent to witness a heartless subhuman culture i-merging i-ven i-mong thee so-called i-ducated groups- thee ME culture. In order to stave off thee sense of crime for our total passivity in thee face of such a great anomaly, at least we should ask ourselves: "What shall we do?" Far-I

Of couse their is a way to liveth wither no monie, if i could bee their i would....Far-i

U sea a be-leaf is a be-leaf we all hold some kinda i-warness unto i-gher Powers, Faith (Future Agricultural Industrial Tiller's Homeland) is trust, that you will bee alright after thee storm, without faith we have no true be-leaf.

Children whom have be-leaf may read Holy scriptures, but overstand thee word not, but i-xcept as a comfort in their day to day lifes at some point, Look upon Rap artist's they often refer to God and thee Word through be-leaf, as too doo KRISTIYAN's go to church, but due too material contamination, thee children are tempted and tested and led astray unto doing wrong, ie Thee Words "Be Fruitfull repelish and multiply"(I-nesis c1 v28) are mere words, wither no content and meaning, are as a empty vessel still re-choir spirit, Spirit is as a strong Rum and "resteth upon I&I River's" also can bee seen upon I&I River's and Oceans if one watches thee tidal waves.

Without content and meaning their is no Devotion, translated Devil, ocean meaning before devocean we are all devil's, Devil meaning Dis-mantled villages in need of spirit of thee Ocean to purify our thoughts, our heart's cleanse and wash i-way our sin's (Simple Injustice's unto Nature)

Without baptism & Immersion in this form, we have not obtained Spirit within it's fullest context, each must bee born unto Water....

Also lies thee word Hope, (Hand of preparing environments) without hope of a better world, we have no plan (Perfect Land)

To obtain Dev-Ocean is a child's freewill (freedom willingness) choice (Choose humanity over iniquity cruelty evil) Evil (Evaporated village igricultural lands)   Self Help (Soul Enthusias Living Freedom Health Enviroment Loving People).

Look upon our Life's we think we have so much, a nice i-partment, city restraints, schools, place's to go, community people, nice job's nice car's a sexual partner, and all i-long we have crumb's.

Can bee seen by thee spiritual eye as four walls, dirty food joint's and a 2 buck disco tech in thee middle of no-where begging for love of one soul partner. In fact 2 people living in a hand made tent, living feasting earthly food's wither a River or Ocean close by would have all one could desire, and this is just thee basic's

A material mind will laugh, as though this was nothing and city living was thee future, Howiver 20 years down thee line, when one is waking i-very day to ask "how much is this" unto thee same shop keeper's in thee same position's One's spirit will supposedly bee dead, and this process can bee called aging, as we waste our youth i-way chasing vanity,and neglect our Health and Love of one I-nother.

We neglect our bodies and mind's by not feeding our spirit's and we I-ventually become prisoner's too one particular i-rea, seaing thee same tings i-very day, unless we are exceedingly wealthy and able too travel as and when we want too, and i-ven so in a material world, nothing much changes i-part from thee weather. To learn of thee earth motherland & Emperor is thee only studie which can offer i-ny real changes.

Far-I

Choice = Choose humanity over Iniquity cruelty evil)

Devotion = Devil ,unto Ocean

Devil = Des-mantled village

Curse = Community Unresponsible Self effort

Evil = Evaporated Village Igricultural Lands

Wicked = Worshipping i-nother countrys Kruelty excel Development

Sin = Simple Injustices unto Nature

Hope =Hand of preparing environments

Plan = Perfect Land

Faith = Future agricultural industrial tiller's Homebound

Black = Be-leaving life advances from cruelty and khaos

White = Willingness to help I&I tidy environment

Negro = National enthusiastic growers rising oversea's

Hell = Handfull everyday's lifes libertys

Command= Community Agricultural National Development

Christ = Casual human Rights ism's sealed untoTafari

7 I&I beloved, Keep I&I words and tresure up my commandments with you;
2 Keep my commandments and liveth, keep my teachings as thee apple of your eye; (PROVERBS 7) Far-I

13. One who despises thee word brings destruction too I-self, but I&I who Ras-pects thee commandment will bee rewarded.
14 Thee teaching of thee wise is a fountain of Life,(Proverbs 13) FAtaR-I

2 , I&I Beloved, if you recieve I&I words and tresure up I&I commandments with you,
2 making your ear to Ittentive to wisdom and inclining your heart too over-standing;
3 yes, if you cry out for insight and raise your voice for overstanding,
4 if you sikh it like silver and search for it as for hidden treasures;
5 then you will overstand thee Loveth of Far-I and find thee knowledge of Far-I thy God.
6 For Far-I giveth's wisdom; from I&I mouth come knowledge and overstanding;
7 I&I stores up sound wisdom for thee upright; I&I is a shield too those who walketh in integrity,
8 guarding thee paths of Justice and preserving thee way of I&I saints.
9 Then you will overstand righteousness and justice and Iquity, Ivery Good path;
10 for wisdom will cometh into your heart, and knowledge will bee pleasant too your soul; (PROVERBS 1) Far-I

Readers Notes

www.ingramcontent.com/pod-product-compliance
Ingram Content Group UK Ltd.
Pitfield, Milton Keynes, MK11 3LW, UK
UKHW020218250726
13967UKWH00001B/61

9 781447 731641